Relief Notes

Encouraging Letters for Tough Times

CHRISTIAN AUTHORS GUILD

Compiled by

Cherise Bopape

When you encounter tough times, may these letters of encouragement help relieve your cares through humor!
Blessings + love,
Debbie
Psalm 118:24

Christian Authors Guild
P. O. Box 2673
Woodstock, GA 30188

www.ChristianAuthorsGuild.org

Printed in the United States of America

DEDICATION

For those experiencing the humbling reality of financial
challenges, the joys and pains of caregiving, and the highs
and lows of overindulgence ... be encouraged.

CONTENTS

PART 2: ADDICTS   **41**

PART 3: FINANCIALLY CHALLENGED   77

ACKNOWLEDGMENTS

Many thanks to our team of editors: Theresa Anderson, Diana J. Baker, and Mary Bowen. Your diligence, insight, and belief in this project shine from cover to cover. Smoothing out the rough edges, you help our words to massage hearts, tickle funny bones, and sparkle.

PART 1

CAREGIVERS

For I was hungry and you gave me something to eat, I was
thirsty and you gave me something to drink, I was a
stranger and you invited me in, I needed clothes and you
clothed me, I was sick and you looked after me, I was in
prison and you came to visit me.
—Matthew 25:35, 36

≈1≈

VISINE USER

Dear Visine User,

  Yes, I can see those red eyes clear from here. You
signed up for something valiant with unintended
consequences. No sleep, frazzled nerves, little empathy,
and you've almost forgotten your first name. The role of
caregiver can be exhausting. I have good news for you.
It's temporary. This isn't permanent. It's a season with a
definable end. That may be hard to locate right now. It's
why the phone somehow got into the freezer and your car
keys were in the bathroom drawer. If you're anything like
me, you volunteered to care for someone you love. Full of
concern, you rose to the task. Perhaps you've discovered
those nearest you don't share your same burden. Signing
up for long days and even longer nights, you may have
asked yourself, "Is this even worth it?" It is.

  Not everyone has a heart large enough to support the
uniform of *The Good Samaritan*. It's a hard choice but filled
with rewards. Your compassionate choice has brought you

close to another's struggle ... to help carry their cross. It allows for growth as you meet someone's basic needs, seeing the depth of their gratitude for your kindness. Sometimes it may be as simple as brushing their hair or placing fresh flowers close enough for them to smell and releasing happy memories of walking through gardens unaided.

Love is an amazing force. It reaches when others withdraw. Its foundation is sacrifice. It rewards the efforts of those motivated by it. When I cared for my aging parents, there were times of complete exhaustion. I longed for relief but chose instead to change my perspective. With my season over, I wouldn't trade a moment. My learned lessons are invaluable, and my parents' final days were easier because I cared for them. Their gratitude was my reward, making regret a stranger. A final hand squeeze was payment in full.

Do something you enjoy. Take a bath, drink a smoothie, watch a movie, or ride your bike. Be kind to yourself and recharge your batteries. A fresh viewpoint grants strength, while loving sacrificially teaches others to do likewise.

Free from regret,

Susan M. Watkins

≈2≈

HUMILIATED 911 CALLER

Dear Humiliated 911 Caller,

I know it's terribly embarrassing to find yourself in a situation where you are helpless and forced to reach out to strangers to rescue you. Somehow, you think it's due to your carelessness or, shall I say it, stupidity. But consider this—no matter what causes your fall from grace—it's best to find the humor in your predicament.

A few years ago, a carefree moment turned to catastrophe. As I carried my lunch to my desk, my toe caught on the carpet. Time slowed as my body (and lunch) did a slow spin. On my way down, my head hit a table and my ankle twisted. I actually saw stars circling above me.

My dachshund came trotting. I thought he planned to comfort me. No, he wanted my lunch! I attempted to get up on my own. No dice. There was no furniture heavy enough to support my weight—or my exploding ankle. I gave in and reached for my phone on the desk above me.

I dialed 911 and said, "I've fallen and I can't get up."

5

Then I giggled. To my relief, the dispatcher chuckled instead of hanging up. I told her what had happened and asked her to send someone strong enough to lift me from the floor. Not wanting my door broken, I added, "There's a stone squirrel in the yard. Tell them to pick it up. A key is hidden in its … butt." We both snorted in laughter.

My goose egg throbbed, but soon my door opened and in walked four of the hunkiest men I had ever seen in my life. They grabbed me, and I was up like a whisper—a one-footed whisper. Why, oh why do these things happen when we are at our worst?

What could have been a quick trip into deep depression became a funny memory. It wouldn't surprise me if God had chuckled a little, too. There is always something positive to dwell on in the worst of moments. Even when you've fallen, He can pick you up.

Giggling on the floor,

Karen Nolan Bell

MOM OF A SPECIAL CHILD

Dear Mom of a Special Child,

Today everyone talks about planning a family, but no one plans to have an imperfect child.

When I was expecting Caleb, I already had four children and also homeschooled. I kept asking the Lord if He really expected me to handle one more child. I don't know how many times I told Him I couldn't count to five. And that was before I realized the huge problems Caleb had.

As a baby, Caleb progressed slowly, but no one noticed because he was so much fun. Before he started walking, we made family pictures. The photographer gathered the family around and put Caleb in a gift box at our feet. The photo was precious—a smiling baby peeking out of a package with a huge bow. We all chuckled when we saw it because it fit. He was born in late December, and I called him my Christmas present. I'm very thankful that imagery stuck with me.

When Caleb was about four, we began to worry about his development. A friend with a degree in education spent some time with him. He told us Caleb had disabilities and that I should start to homeschool him also. I soon discovered how difficult it was for him to learn even the simplest tasks.

The constant struggle had a huge impact on Caleb. Now that he's in his twenties, he's gracious and compassionate. If something bad happens or if we feel sad, he's the first to notice. And he always offers an encouraging word. If anyone visits his Sunday school class, Caleb's the first to greet him and make him feel comfortable. He never forgets to compliment the pastor's sermon and often reminds me about birthdays on Facebook. His jokes catch us by surprise, and he loves to send silly text messages, especially about gummy bears, his favorite treat.

Now I can't imagine life without my Caleb. He's the best Christmas present besides Jesus I ever received.

Each infant God creates comes with a special blessing. Look for the one God gave your child.

Praising God for His gift,

Cynthia L. Simmons

≈4≈

CONCERNED CAREGIVER

Dear Concerned Caregiver,

As I have seen my brother Bob suffering through the many indignities and losses of stage 4 colon cancer, how I want to "make it all better" for him.

As a former cancer patient, I can identify with part of his struggle. I'm so glad we can visit together often and be honest about our feelings. We both need to process our emotions.

We draw strength and hope from Scripture as Bob shares passages that have helped him. Soaking in the life-giving words nourishes our flagging spirits. When we're together, I avoid clichés like "all you need is faith," "praise the Lord anyway," and "don't worry – God loves you." Although I know God is our healer and is in control and working all things for our good, Bob doesn't need platitudes. Instead, I listen to his words with my heart and absorb their emotion. To feel understood is a healing balm.

I want to help bear the burden of his serious illness, but I try not to identify with him so much that I'm unable to help. I take care of myself as a caregiver. One way is to exercise. I take an aerobics class three times weekly, which always strengthens my spirits along with my abs. Taking trips is another means of recreating. Last April my husband and I flew out to the mountains of Utah to ski on that dazzling, powdery snow. I came back limping, but refreshed. (Remember to preserve your own mobility in your great escapes!)

I also regroup by reading and meditating in a quiet natural setting. I often journal my thoughts and prayers while in that "oasis." To defuse my anger or frustration, I talk with girlfriends in person or on the phone. This is an effective safety net.

When I visit with Bob, I know God is there with us, cushioning the harshness. Our shared faith and our personal history together bond us, giving hope. I see God's power in Bob's weakness as he graciously accepts his limitations, trusts the Lord's character, and still makes me laugh with his jokes.

Cared-for Caregiver,

Mary Bowen

≈6≈

MARRED MAMA

Dear Marred Mama,

We share a great love for our strong-willed children, yet their headstrong personalities once exhausted us. The grueling day-to-day clashes wore us out to the point that we prayed they might be blessed with a child just like themselves. Through a grandchild, we now find our prayers have been answered.

I've raised a son and a daughter whom I dearly love. My husband traveled in his job while I worked as a stay-at-home mom. Rarely did I escape my job. From sunup to sundown and beyond, my job literally stared me in the face. Sometimes my charges exuded happiness, while at other times, they exhibited tears and in-fighting. Most every day my little boy expressed a strong will and it took fortitude to raise him.

You, too, possibly jumped hurdles and fought battles. Did you discover which struggles to contend with? The tug of war taught me which conflicts to fight in order to train up a spirited and respectful young man. What a challenge! I'm sure we both begged, "Please God, give them children like themselves."

How could I have known the power of my prayers? As a mother, I simply voiced my momentary frustrations. As a grandmother, now a generation later, I've learned a thing or two and tend to lament certain decisions I once made.

Why did I pray that prayer? As a fairly new grandmother, I see my son's unbending nature in his little daughter. How she pushes to the point of no return! I regret the wish for revenge, especially since there's another person involved—my daughter-in-law. I feel for my son and his wife as they contend with a determined personality. So my prayer has changed, and I hope yours has too. I say, "Dear Lord, I'm thankful for the strong-willed character of my son because he will be able to handle his daughter."

I've relinquished some of my mothering and taken a back seat to my children as they raise their own children; maybe you have as well. As grandmothers, we offer support and loving prayers while concealing our smiles.

Renovated Nana,

Deborah Crawford

≈7≈

CONCERNED FLORENCE NIGHTINGALES

Dear Concerned Florence Nightingales,

I didn't mean to be Florence Nightingale. I was thrown into the picture!

As my friend and I walked onto the porch of our favorite Woodstock restaurant, a charming tea room, we saw Kim, the owner, picking pansies. We hadn't even completed our "hellos" when screeching brakes and a loud crash made our heads jerk toward the street. Our eyes widened with fear!

A motorcycle rider had slammed into an SUV waiting in the line of backed-up traffic. He lay in the street amid scattered debris. We thought he was dead.

Kim, still holding the pansies, walked toward the street. She repeatedly hollered, "Are you all right?" The rider lay still. As Kim neared the road, the man suddenly hopped up, circled around a couple times, righted his motorcycle, and with a curse, laboriously pushed it to the side street to allow the traffic to move.

Kim shouted, "The SUV left! They just drove off!" They *had*. The driver had left, not getting out of his vehicle and not knowing if the rider had died or whether the back of his SUV had received damages.

I headed for the road. My friend yelled, "Where are you going?" I couldn't wait. I had to see for myself that the biker was all right. His curse words had set me off.

The young man had parked his motorcycle. Looking dazed, he slowly removed his helmet. I asked, "Are you okay?"

He flexed his hands, shook his legs, smiled, and said, "I'm okay."

"If I were you, when I got home tonight, I'd get on my knees and thank the Lord for blessing me today," I said. "We thought you were dead."

In response, he casually pushed his cycle to the parking lot to check it out.

After we were finally seated in the tea room, Kim came and thanked me for being so nice to the young man. *What? I hadn't been nice. I had only been concerned.*

"We didn't intend to make such a *crashing* entry," I said. We both smiled in grateful relief.

A thankful "watcher,"

June Parks

≈8≈

WAITING

Dear Waiting,

The waiting room is a lonely place. Our minds have time to wander, making way for a multitude of thoughts and feelings all colliding and vying for center stage.

After weeks of travel, I phoned Aunt Nellie, my mom's elder sister for whom I held power of attorney and had committed to care for while waiting for her scheduled surgery. I asked Aunt Nellie if I could delay coming until I worshiped at my church. She affirmed, but her faltering voice denied her response. I packed my dirty laundry and headed to her home. When I arrived, she blurted, "Now you can make all the decisions." Not what I was prepared for.

Pending the outcome of her cancer surgery, we discussed her wishes and talked frankly about her trust in God. The day we left for the hospital, her siblings—minus my mom who was serving as a missionary in England—came to see her off. In the hospital, Aunt Nellie aspirated

17

and was rushed to CCU. The circumstances tested my ability to wait.

The surgical team told me my aunt was no longer a candidate for surgery. Her kidneys were shutting down. They wanted to surgically insert stents in her kidneys, and repeat it every three months. I asked the doctor if this were his mom would he choose to do the stents. He responded, "No." With that news, we left via medical transport to go to our previously scheduled rehab center.

Aunt Nellie settled into rehab, but in reality she received palliative care. We all joined in waiting as my aunt lived out her last days. Several times we prayed Aunt Nellie on to heaven, only to have her brown eyes pop open. I phoned my mom in England and explained the situation. "If you want to see your sister this side of heaven, you need to come now." They shared a brief visit the evening of Mom's arrival and the next afternoon my aunt made her transition to glory.

My family's waiting then became joyful, because we knew Aunt Nellie's declaration of faith and her eternal destiny.

Resting assured,

Sue Schultz

≈9≈

HEALTH CHALLENGED

Dear Health Challenged,

I know we both spend more time sitting in waiting rooms than we prefer. Let's be honest, long waits surrounded by fellow sickies are boring.

One day, as I waited—and waited—for my turn to see yet another medical professional who most likely would not find an answer to my latest issue, I perused the other waiting patients. A cloud hung over the room. I wondered why each person was there. Was it something as minor as a cold or as frightening as a need for surgery? Was the young mother pregnant for the third time in three years? Did her mammogram come back with a suspicious anomaly? Was the man staring at his shoes because he suspected his doctor would tell him about the "C" word today? I wondered how many were facing debilitating diseases, chronic illness, expensive treatments they couldn't afford, or no diagnosis of why they were deteriorating.

In their eyes, I sensed the fear, worry, weariness, and

hopelessness I have experienced myself as my chronic illnesses have progressed. The darkness hung over me, too.

I whimpered, *No, Lord! This isn't fair. Why do we have to be miserable? Why can't You heal us? Why can't You fix us or give us hope?*

A response popped into my head: *You are here to be the ray of hope for just one person.*

With the intent of ignoring the prompt, I looked at the woman across from me as she held a book in her hands, unopened. She met my gaze and I surrendered. I smiled and said, "What book are you reading? Is it any good?"

A conversation began as we discussed the book. Then I suggested a couple of books she might enjoy. We regaled one another with news of our children, grandchildren, the weather, our doctors, and traffic. Those sitting nearby joined the chat as we shared anecdotes and funny stories, including our doctors' quirks.

As the nurses called each of us back, we carried a smile with us. The fog had dissipated and the room seemed brighter. I had become an "accidental caregiver" to one person, and the Lord had multiplied it, just like the loaves and fishes. Next time you're in a similar situation, reach out and be a ...

Giver of Smiles,

Karen Nolan Bell

≈10≈

OREO FLUFF

Dear Oreo Fluff,

You are the soft center between two cookies; a member of the sandwich generation, smashed between teenagers and aging parents who both depend on you. It's tough providing care for one, but both at once can banish your sweetness. Like you, I was constantly challenged by their reactions to four difficult Ds.

1. **Driving:** I gave the car keys to my teenagers with trepidation. I worried and prayed when they weren't home by the designated time. When my father got behind the wheel, I feared for other drivers. I had ridden with him enough to observe his slowed reaction time. It was not easy for him to give up his keys when it was time.

2. **Doctors:** Both my sons and my mother had asthma. I took them to doctors with different results. My sons hated the medication and breathing treatments but followed doctor's orders. My mother

chose to self-medicate, ignoring the treatment plan and ending up in the hospital.

3. **Decisions:** As the Oreo fluff, I walked gently to encourage good decision making. It was a battle of wills with me in the middle. My sons assumed I was an old fogey who couldn't understand a teenager. My aging parents resented the role reversal and were determined to sabotage every arrangement I made for their care.

4. **Discarding:** My sons had no desire to keep clean rooms. Their collections of baseball cards and childhood toys overwhelmed their space. Likewise, pleas to my mother-in-law to begin sorting a lifetime of clutter fell on deaf ears. A discarded scrap was often retrieved from the trash. Her stuff was like a wall built to keep everyone out.

I realize now how much God was teaching me. As my patience was tried, my prayer life became more fervent, and I learned valuable lessons.

Our children, with families of their own, will one day care for us. Let's start now to unclutter our lives, make good decisions about our health and future, and willingly open our hands to accept any help they offer.

Mrs. Good Cookie,

Frieda Dixon

≈11≈

MOTHER OF A MINI ME

Dear Mother of a Mini Me,

Are you feeling rejected by your daughter? Do her unkind words stab your heart? Does your relationship seem hopeless? At one time I answered "yes" to these questions, but I write to encourage you with hope for brighter times ahead.

When my daughter reached her early teens, I noticed her rolling eyes when her lips spouted sass. Through high school, the explanations of her comings and goings were like bits of fiction made for television. In college, her actions mimicked an insurgent of the Revolutionary War as she rebelled against the directives of the mother country. A war of words ensued.

As I wondered how our lives misfired, I recognized myself reflected in her face. Gazing into a mirror, I found myself staring at my mother. Oh the bonds of family ties!

Haunting words nagged at me as I remembered my own spewing lips responding to my parents, "No, I'm not going. I'd rather stay at home than be seen in public with you!" Then I recalled a Christmas past when my daughter planned to return to college early rather than stay home throughout her break.

Explaining these events to my mom triggered an inner smile, as she quietly sat back and watched the light bulb go off in my head. Who could blame her for releasing a heavy sigh? Maybe one day I'll get a chance to see evidence of an "aha" moment from my daughter when she experiences the similar burdens of motherhood.

My duty as mother has finally transformed from being the enemy to being the friend who gives advice when life goes wrong, bills aren't paid, or sickness strikes. My role as daughter is fast becoming caregiver to my aging mother who braves physical ailments and disease.

There may be occasional battles between us mothers and daughters, but the war is over and peace reigns. Love for each other fills our hearts. Time and prayer have healed most of our wounds, so I urge you to pray for your daughter and persevere in loving her. If you look hard enough, I believe you can spot a white flag over the horizon.

Once caught in the middle,

Deborah Crawford

≈12≈

AILING RELATIVES

Dear Ailing Relatives,

Almost nine months ago, I accepted the position of caretaker for Sarah, my aging mother-in-law. It began with a call from the local police who informed me that Sarah had been calling them nightly. She had reported someone prowling around her apartment, sleeping on her porch, and shining laser beams under her bed. By the time the police contacted me, she had racked up twenty-six 911 calls in less than a month. After the call from the police, Sarah was admitted to a hospital for evaluation.

Soon my days were filled with talking to social workers, nurses, and admissions personnel about dementia, nursing homes, and a lack of resources. I spent four frantic and frustrating months trying to find an appropriate placement for Sarah. It was like trying to connect with a moving target. After three different hospital admissions and two different nursing homes, she finally seems to have found a place she can call home.

I've learned a lot from this season of service. Some are practical things like getting my finances in order and the importance of making a living will. There are also the intangible things such as the value of love and toughing it out during the impossibly hard times when there seem to be no options.

I'm grateful for friends I can lean on for emotional support and wisdom. When possible, I return the favor and share my experience with others who find themselves in a similar position. Most importantly, I've developed the patience to let God's plan unfold even when I am filled with doubt and despair.

Although I'm thankful for the opportunity to serve my family, I'm looking forward to simply fulfilling my role as daughter-in-law. Perhaps then, I can more aptly care for another important individual … me.

Believing better days are ahead,

Lynne Watts

≈13≈

SONS SERVING FATHERS

Dear Sons Serving Fathers,

I tucked him in, turned down the TV, and turned off the lights. I gave him his nightly dose of morphine. He would sleep now, but the night would be anything but restful. The hospice nurses had called the effects of morphine "the death rattle." I watched and listened for a bit as my father drifted into slumber.

Later in the nearby bedroom, with the door slightly open, I lay quietly with my eyes closed and my ears alert. On other nights, I would awaken to my dad's groaning. These sounds were part of the "rattle."

This night, I awoke to him calling my name. I leapt out of bed and ran to his bedside. He lay on his back crying.

"I wet myself," he sniffled.

"Hey, that's okay," I said, trying to comfort him. "I'll get you some dry underwear."

I knew what I had to do, but had never done it before. My dad couldn't move while under the drug influence. I

27

was tired and frazzled, but still managed to find some clean underwear for him.

Then I stood at the end of his bed, peeling back wet sheets and pulling off soaked shorts by the light of the soundless TV. When the Bible calls us to honor our parents, I believe it has nothing to do with parents commanding their kids to obey. Instead, it has everything to do with caring for our parents when the world no longer considers them honorable.

As I tugged to remove a sheet, Dad rolled to the edge of the bed. I stretched my arms out to catch him. He stared up at me, his eyes wide with fright.

"It's okay," I said. "Don't you know I love you too much to let you fall?" His body relaxed, and his eyes closed again. The death rattle had been silenced for a time. Hope returned in the new morning.

From death rattle to morning hope,

M. L. Anderson

≈14≈

HOPEFUL AFTER HEART ATTACK

Dear Hopeful After Heart Attack,

That hospital scared me. Heart attack hurt. Recovery was worse. Wires dangled from my chest in case they had to jolt me back to life again.

Glad folks came to visit, though it turned into a regular circus in my room: kinfolk, neighbors, nurses, parsons, and strangers. Got so's I couldn't tell one from another.

Horace and Lucille visited me on Saturday. That's when it happened. During the idle palaver leading up to lunch, a most handsome woman walked into the room. Her blond hair was pulled back by a dark ribbon. Her soft gray eyes held my own as if nothing else was going on in this world.

I'd never seen her before, but I could tell she was a doctor. It was stitched right there above the pocket of her lab coat. She asked me to breathe for her while I sat bent over in bed. She listened through that stethoscope, and we were almost cheek to cheek.

Her beauty practically lit up the room. Horace stood there mouth open, saying nothing. I could genuinely feel the warmth of her radiance on my face.

So finally I asked her, "How's it look for me, Doc?" She didn't answer at once. Then she leaned in close, putting a hand on my shoulder. "It's looking good. Keep it positive." In another minute she was gone.

Later on, I had to traipse out to the surgeon's office, and on another day made it over to the heart doctor's building. I asked about that lady doctor, but nobody at those two places had ever heard of her. Same story from the head nurse that ran my floor at Memorial General.

When I told the preacher this curious tale, he asked me, "A personage of great beauty? But a brief encounter? And you were told good news?" When I nodded "yes," he smiled. "Son, that's how some would describe an angel."

Now she may be, and she may not. Don't care. Until the Lord says otherwise, I'll claim her as MY guardian angel.

Touched by an angel,

T. W. Lawrence

≈15≈

SANDWICHED BETWEEN

Dear Sandwiched Between,

Being in the middle of both heel ends of a loaf—caring for a helpless parent and handling responsibilities as a single mom—can become drudgery unless one uses creative ways to make it fun.

My mom, physically impaired with multiple sclerosis (MS), fell and fractured her hip. She had surgery and post-op traction. Three months later, she transferred to a nursing facility. Since Medicaid did not cover a rehabilitation center, and due to MS, her hopes of learning to walk again were severely diminished.

My daughter Debbie and I visited Mom every day after I left work. We learned to exist on a diet of fast food sandwiches for an entire year. Talk about being the sandwich generation! We did, however, manage home cooked meals on weekends.

Mom had many needs not met by in-house caretakers, so I emptied bedpans, changed sheets, and dressed Mom

31

with a fresh gown every day. I took her soiled gowns home to wash for the next day.

One evening Mom was weary from sitting up in bed; staff had failed to answer the call bell. Relieved to see me, she asked me to lower her bed. Walking to the foot of the bed, with my back to Mom and Debbie, I started cranking. Suddenly, I heard a duet of frightened voices yelling, "Stop!" I spun around and there was Mom looking petrified, almost completely sandwiched in the folded mattress. I had used the wrong crank. Once I returned her to a prone position, I joked, "*I'm* supposed to be the sandwich generation."

The mishap gave us all a hearty laugh and also became grapevine news repeated for nurses, family members, and visitors. It got more of a hoot than the senile men streaking down the hallways without their gowns!

We may not foresee what might bring a smile to our faces or tears to our eyes from laughing so hard. Nor can we know what precious memories will be shared across generational divides.

On behalf of the courageous three,

Laura Garron Havens

≈16≈

PREACHER MAN

Dear Preacher Man,

I retraced my steps out of the huge double doors as church ended. I headed for the sunshine bearing down on the columned front porch of the First Methodist Church. Downtown Marietta could be viewed from that porch. The tall spire above our heads was a beacon for worshipers from all quarters of the county and beyond.

As I approached the door, the preacher in his long, heavy vestments had foot traffic backed up, as he made sure all comers were greeted and welcomed. With his sermons, he touched a lot of spots in parishioners' souls that needed stirring. I knew he touched me. He was a good preacher and a good man.

One sunny Sunday as I neared, he grabbed my hand with a smile, but suddenly he gave his attention to a former politician and his wife in line ahead of me. I'm sure their donations to fill the church's coffers prompted the preacher's attention and friendliness.

These people were both huge—tall and overweight. They laughed and socialized, holding up the line of greeters. The two of them filled the space.

The preacher continued to hold my hand and even pulled it up to his chest, cradling it with both his comforting hands. I wondered how his hands could be so soft. He surely must take out the trash and do a few chores. I knew he performed a lot of funerals and visitations, possible note-writing, or telephoning. But his hands were not at all work-hardy. They were a comfort.

His warm heartfelt, caregiving gesture nearly brought tears to my eyes. It meant nothing to him, his attention being elsewhere, but his hands holding mine warmed my soul. I didn't know it, but at that moment I needed that feeling. He could not have done more had he hugged me. I felt loved.

I needed that! Sometimes, it is the *little* things that we do that give a warm feeling to someone. We may never know what impact it makes. A smile is small, but can be a people-mover. A handshake is a personal touch. It can mean a lot!

Passing along warmth,

June Parks

≈17≈

POOPED-OUT PARENT

Dear Pooped-Out Parent,

Are you tired, run-down, listless? Lucille Ball, in her TV show, offered a liquid containing vitamins, meats, vegetables, and minerals as a cure. But only sleep will help you! I know because we share an undesired alliance—lack of sleep due to fussy babies.

While most of the world prepared for slumber, I cared for a baby who only dozed. Oh, how I yearned for a bit of shut-eye! After getting him settled, I would stealthily creep off to bed. Just as I closed one eye, a cry would pierce the quiet night. "Awake again," I would say with a sigh.

I completely understand your double life as a night owl and an early bird. Years ago I shrieked nightly with the best of those owls as I wearily tried to feed and comfort my crying baby. Daily the sun arose to find us already up with the birds, twittering our morning melody.

Routinely, my son woke up around 2 a.m. and again at 5:30 a.m., after having gone to bed late in the evening.

Deciding we simply couldn't live a sleep-deprived life, my husband and I attempted to turn a deaf ear to his howling. One night we heard strange sounds coming from his room and discovered our 14-month-old trying to climb out of his crib. What determination!

Fearing he would fall from the top of his crib, we replaced the crib with a used trundle bed which can be rolled under its larger twin. Anxiety over our toddler's safety ceased, but our insomnia did not. He could easily crawl out of bed and join us.

"No rest for the weary" became my mantra. Fatigued, I continually prayed, "Oh Lord, give me a power nap!" God strengthened me as I napped through those years. Trust Him to do the same for you and learn to enjoy your child. The weary memories eventually turn to smiles.

Retiring early,

Deborah Crawford

≈18≈

BEWILDERED CAT LOVERS

Dear Bewildered Cat Lovers,

I recently chatted with my favorite feline, Miss Bijoux. She expressed concern about her declining health, and I wanted to share her comments to help you understand your own aging cats better:

> I see your worried looks and hear your whispered comments. You're wondering what's become of your former frisky feline. The spring in my step has slowed to a pronounced limp. My lustrous white fur doesn't shine anymore; it's yellowed, oily, and matted. When you stroke my back, you feel my bones. The truth is, I'm old.
>
> Thank you for a wonderful life. Over time I've seen my feral contemporaries come and quickly go. Your loving care has extended my years exponentially. It's been a long run, but now it's coming to an end.

As we transition into this final phase of my life, let me share a few thoughts. Forgive me if I miss the litter box. I'm not as limber and it's difficult to squat. Sorry about the hairballs and sudden bouts of nausea; my digestive system's grown temperamental with age. My cries in the night aren't meant to keep you up; they're my way to grieve for the life I see disappearing.

Finally, I ask that you place my need for a swift, peaceful passing over your own feelings of loss. Please, no heroics to prolong my life. When it's time, release me. This will be the greatest gift you can give your dear friend.

As time winds down, I'm confident that we'll all adjust to these changes. I want you to know you're loved and appreciated not only for all you've done, but especially for who you are!

We pet lovers all face tough decisions as our animals age. Years of companionship have endeared them to us as beloved family members. But their health and welfare should take precedence over our desire to hold on. We can repay their years of faithful devotion with a peaceful and painless departure. They'll appreciate our final act of love.

Wishing you purrfect peace,

Mary Agrusa

≈19≈

CARING

Dear Caring,

My precious nine-year-old grandson is a caring little guy. I wanted you to hear about him. His name is Cole, but I call him Coley. He is an energetic, wonderful, thoughtful boy with lots of curiosity. He is a trusting soul and approves of everyone and nearly all that they do.

My niece, Cheryl, lives in snowy Denver and gets to Georgia very seldom, so it is a big thing when she visits. When Cheryl comes, we welcome her with open arms. The last time she came, Cole had not seen her in many years and had no recollection of her. However, when he met her, he immediately fell in love.

A whole gang of our local family members went to dinner that Friday night to celebrate Cheryl's visit. We nearly filled up a local Italian restaurant, circling around a huge food-laden table in the center of the room. Our laughter and loud conversations had to have disturbed all the other patrons, but for us, it was a celebration.

Laughing and talking all at once, we sounded like real Italians! Cole sat beside Cheryl holding on to every word that fell from her pretty lips. He hardly ate.

Cheryl waited as long as possible then had to excuse herself. She went outside on the front sidewalk to smoke. Cole, Mr. Inquisitive, accompanied Cheryl and my daughter-in-law, Terri, outside. He wanted to chat and get better acquainted with Cheryl.

Cheryl, trying to mentor Cole, said, "I just came out to smoke. I wish I didn't. It is my bad habit. I'm trying to quit. I think I am going to get hypnotized so I will quit."

Cole piped up with his handy, friendly expertise and said, "You don't need to be hypnotized. You need to be baptized. I have a friend in my class at school who cussed all the time. He got baptized. Cut that cussing right in half!"

Out of the mouths of babes,

June Parks

PART 2

ADDICTS

No temptation has seized you except what is common to man. And God is faithful; he will not let you be tempted beyond what you can bear. But when you are tempted, he will also provide a way out so that you can stand up under it.

—1 Corinthians 10:13

≈20≈

BOOK-BUYING BOOKAHOLIC

Dear Book-Buying Bookaholic,

You and I share the obsession of buying books, yet not necessarily reading them. Whether we are in big-name, used, or online bookstores, our weakness for purchasing books surfaces until we can't fight it anymore and out pop our wallets. It's not such a bad habit to buy informative material, right?

Excitement courses within me when I approach a bookstore. As I open the door, an aromatic bouquet of wood pulp from spruce, pine, eucalyptus, and birch trees engulfs me. I see only a forest of trees as I trek through rows of books. My fingers stroke the many volumes until I uncover an intriguing selection and leaf through its pages. TIMBER! A book falls into my hand and goes home with me.

Not only do I enjoy strolling through a brick-and-mortar bookstore, I also enjoy perusing websites. I scan the web page, select my favorite choices, pay with a credit card, and wait for about a week. A package of books arrives at my front door, and I can hardly wait to unwrap my purchase.

Though I love to read, I've encountered various problems with my addiction. Several rooms in my house bulge with overloaded bookshelves. My cabinets are stuffed to overflowing, and many volumes are piled on the floor. If only I had enough time to read them all!

One day my husband asked, "Why do you continue to buy so many books?"

I answered, "Because people keep writing them."

I'm afraid to admit to a personal problem, but the reality is, I'm a book-buying junkie. It's possible I could star in a TV reality show as a book hoarder.

Whew! Finally, I've taken the first step—admitting my problem. Maybe you and I could begin sharing books instead of buying them. We might even donate books to a nursing home, school, or church. I already see space opening up in my home! Do you have any empty bookshelves yet?

Pressed between the pages,

Deborah Crawford

≈21≈

FELLOW COLLECTOR

Dear Fellow Collector,

Little did my parents know when they gave me their empty matchbook covers decorated with birds, butterflies, animals, and flowers that they were setting me up for a lifelong addiction.

In fact, my parents actually encouraged me to collect things. They saw collecting as a fun hobby, not an addiction. And since they had acquired few things while growing up in the Great Depression, they had begun collections of their own—which I inherited when they passed away.

My childhood collections included post cards, pop beads, four-leaf clovers, dolls, stuffed animals, and small glass figurines. Although I still have some of those things, most of my stuffed animals and figurines bit the dust, and my four-leaf clovers turned to dust almost fifty years ago.

During my junior high and high school years, my friends and I got caught up in the silver charm collecting craze. By the time that fad ended, I had so many charms on my bracelet I could barely lift my arm when I wore it.

After I married, I continued to collect. I started collections for my four children and, later in life, for my grandchildren. Today my collections of kitchen antiques, fast food collectibles, antique cameras, children's books, dolls, beanbag toys, and paintings fill our three-story, five-bedroom home.

Although collections take up space, I don't believe they are intrinsically wrong. After all, God Himself created the beautiful wildlife, plants, and scenery that inspired them. A problem arises when collecting becomes an addiction that takes over our thoughts, time, finances, and living space. It *is* sinful when our collections become more important to us than our relationship with God and others.

I pray that we will grow deeper in our daily fellowship with the Lord, that our desire for Him will overpower our desire to acquire stuff, and that He will inspire us with creative ways to use our hobby to bless others.

A reforming collector,

Diana J. Baker

≈22≈

CHOCOLATE INDUCED COMA

Dear Chocolate Induced Coma,

I understand your position. I too have rarely met something chocolate I didn't like. When life is good, I celebrate with my favorite treat. When life goes south, what better comforter than my favorite food group? I've lived by my golden, or should I say, dark brown semi-sweet, rule: I'd give up chocolate, but I'm no quitter.

Chocolate speaks to me. Leftover birthday cake calls out, "Come, indulge. Enjoy a piece for breakfast, lunch, and dinner." I willingly oblige. Toll House cookies clamor for my attention amidst fruits and vegetables. Fat chance I'll choose substance over sweets. Chocolate ice cream covered in chocolate syrup transforms my coffee into an instant dessert. Yum.

Oh, I know your friend intimately—and I caution you. The relationship you have teeters on the brink of obsession. Years of running with this rascal left me breathless, not from euphoric experiences, but weight gain.

I huffed and puffed as I lifted another tasty morsel to my mouth. Chocolate is not our friend.

Here are some tips I've learned to set boundaries and rein in the chocolate monster:

1. Donate all your stash to a food bank, preferably one that feeds your enemies. They'll be hard pressed to chase you as they pile on the pounds.

2. Duct tape is a less expensive alternative to wiring your mouth shut. Be sure to leave your nose uncovered; no need to resist unto death.

3. Exercise. I'm talking about real calorie-burning exertion. Rumor has it that the endorphin rush of a hard workout rivals that of a bag of chocolate covered espresso beans. The jury is still out on that one.

Finally, remember this is a temporary separation, not a divorce. Let's determine how much of a good thing is sufficient. We can resume our love of chocolate according to our parameters; this places us in control and not in a coma.

The Milky Way Mama,

Mary Agrusa

≈23≈

MARRIED TO A CONTROL FREAK

Dear Married to a Control Freak,

After a month of marriage, I realized I had married a control freak. The first week, he complained about my squeezing the toothpaste in the middle. Then he said I turned the toilet paper upside down on the holder. Now, I grew up in Appalachia, so I had never used a toilet paper holder on the wall. How was I to know?

Piles of mail, reading materials, and books soon appeared on every piece of furniture and then spread to the floor. He refused to pick them up and put them where they belonged. He also refused to organize his clothing according to color in the closet. It boggled my mind how he could possibly get dressed in the morning without color coordinating his suits, shirts, ties, and socks the night before. He was determined to frustrate me with his disorganization.

Even mealtime challenged me. He refused to take his plate to the kitchen, rinse it, and put it in the dishwasher.

Instead, he insisted upon leaving everything on the table. His insensitivity drove me to distraction.

Over the years, he exhibited his control countless times by insisting on doing everything his own way instead of in the sensible, mature way. My life was a constant frustration.

One particularly miserable day, his control issues drove me to tearful prayer. I had tried for years to change my husband's misdirected lifestyle and teach him to give up his dominance over all aspects of my life. As I prayed, I sensed God's gentle voice telling me, *Karen, you are the control freak. The only way you—or your hubby—can ever change is if you allow Me to be the changer.*

That was the day I stopped trying to change my husband and gave it over to the Lord. Guess what. We both changed—a little. Unfortunately, old ways sometimes creep back into my life, and my controlling ways reach out for new victims.

Are you having the same problem? Just remember: we can't change anyone but ourselves. So, give everyone, self included, to God. He'll do the changing.

Not such a freak,

Karen Nolan Bell

≈24≈

SCARED SILLY

Dear Scared Silly,

This world is a dangerous place. If you aren't careful, you could find yourself locked within the four walls of your home, gripped with fear.

Even within the relative safety of your home there are things to be feared. For example, my lovely wife is deathly afraid of mice. She has had several encounters with the furry creatures and has found herself standing on a chair or a bed to avoid Mickey, Minnie, Mighty, or one of their cousins.

One year we took a mission trip to Canada and our team stayed in cabins at a youth camp. Being concerned with the possible danger of stepping on her nemesis, my wife insisted on having several traps set and scattered on the floor of the cabin as a precaution. The next morning while she was in the shower, one of the girls discovered that the four-legged creature had met its demise. As this girl tried to discreetly remove and dispose of the body, my wife stepped from the shower and nearly ran into her. A few tense moments ensued until another young lady distracted my wife.

Once when our daughter and her family were visiting us, my wife discovered mouse droppings in the kitchen. Being the fearless hunter, I gathered my braves together and went on the prowl for the wild beast. We cornered it behind the refrigerator where it fought back valiantly. My wife cheered us on from the safety of a chair. When we captured our prize, we paraded our trophy around the room as female shrieks echoed off the walls.

In time, my wife came to realize that the shadow loomed larger than the substance of her fear. Of course, we should beware when facing a potentially dangerous situation. Nevertheless, we often let little things grow out of proportion until we're immobilized by what is relatively benign. So take heart, oh fearful one. The shadow cast across your path may bring a moment's pause, but only run to safety's shore when you can see its claws.

Mighty Mouse Slayer,

Bryan M. Powell

≈25≈

NAIL-BITER

Dear Nail-Biter,

Fingers to the mouth, you unconsciously chew until you find there's nothing left. Your nails are gone, revealing bare nubs at the end of bleeding fingers. Diagnosis: classic nail-biter.

You've tried all the tricks, including painting your nails with nasty tasting guaranteed cures, to no avail. Every waking moment is a struggle to refrain from the constant biting.

Nail-biting was a challenge for my granddaughter Jewel because she wanted long fingernails to polish. Her daddy is a nail-biter and so is her older brother. Even her mom struggled as a child with chewing her nails. Jewel has a heritage of nail-biting.

Jewel asked her mom for help. Together they polished her nails with pretty pink polish. Her mom continued to gently remind Jewel of her desire for longer nails. A few times her mom bought her fake nails to show her what it would be like to have long nails. When Jewel was a little older, her mom took her to a nail salon to have her nails decorated with flowers and rhinestones. Jewel was delighted.

As Jewel set out to master her nail-biting, she had to own her difficulty. She asked for help, and with her mother's assistance, they took proactive steps to stop her nail-biting. Today she sports a lovely manicure along with her pretty pedicure … no more nail-biting.

Researchers report that it takes twenty-one days to make a new habit or to break a bad one. Consistency on the twenty-one day journey is what makes it difficult.

Like my granddaughter, I've tried to start a new habit, such as dieting, only to fall off the wagon and have to try again. But when the Lord remade a habit into a personal victory for me, He did so completely. May the Lord continue to remake us all until we are victorious.

Victorious Ex-Nail-Biter,

Sue Schultz

≈26≈

SPEED ADDICT

Dear Speed Addict,

"Time is money," and we both want to use it wisely. Sometimes, our to-do lists seem to issue a silent challenge for us to conquer them by the end of the day. It's fun to compete against ourselves as we watch the clock and see how fast we can get things done. But it can be so frustrating when we get on the road, especially when driving to work. Those slow drivers bother me, too, not to mention all the red lights and stop signs. Why is there always an obstacle to progress?

I remember one night years ago when I was driving home after a party. I've never been a night owl, and it was close to midnight. I could hardly keep my eyes open. *Almost there … why did that light have to turn red so close to home?* I thought. Nobody else was even on the road except for one car behind me. Impatiently, I flipped on my blinker and started to turn left. A siren suddenly screeched in my ears. I squinted as blue lights flashed in my rearview mirror. *Uh, oh.* As I pulled over, a policewoman got out, shaking her head. "I can't believe you did that!" she exclaimed. I couldn't believe it, either.

When I'm in a rush, not only does my good judgment falter, but I also miss the pleasures of the moment. If I'm pressured with a project, I try to pace myself with "mini-breaks." Calling a friend, reading a chapter or two in a favorite book, or walking in the yard to enjoy our garden all refresh me. Another way I slow down is by taking time to read God's Word and pray. His presence throughout the day grounds me in His timeless peace as I realize that my time is actually a gift from Him.

Savoring my moments,

Mary Bowen

≈27≈

HIGH AND DRY

Dear High and Dry,

Are you stressed to the max with no relief in sight? When life hands me more than I can take, I head for the water. I am addicted to the liquid therapy of H_2O.

Shower power provides me with a new perspective. The warm water flows over my body, washing away my cares and giving me time to think. I create the next line of my latest writing project. I make a mental list of my priorities for the day. And I pray for folks needing a healing touch. After a long while, my husband often shouts through the door, "Have you washed down the drain yet?" That's when I know it's time to stop daydreaming and get busy.

Another perk after an overloaded few hours of work is a rejuvenating sip of tea. I fill the electric water pot, select my favorite herbal tea, and eagerly wait for it to brew. A hot cup of tea provides a respite in a hectic schedule. Maybe the British are on to something after all. Holding a cup of tea requires me to sit and sip and relax as the hot liquid infuses my soul with refreshment.

But the best tranquilizer of all is a strenuous hour of aquatic exercise. Though my swim group is called "The Mermaids," we lack long blond hair and the svelte bodies of our youth. We all wear flotation belts as the instructor leads us through a vigorous routine. I'm sure my blood pressure must drop as I pump my legs and arms to the music. How relaxed I feel, and I look forward to a good night's sleep.

Up to 80% of our body weight is water. No wonder we respond so well to this natural remedy. The next time you find yourself needing a pause that refreshes, don't reach for pills or potions; just pick your favorite H_2O therapy and say "Ahhh."

Soaked but soothed,

Frieda Dixon

≈28≈

JEZEBEL BRIDE

Dear Jezebel Bride,

After wedding the pig farmer, birthing two terrific sons, divorcing the pig farmer, and then losing my precious mother to cancer, this single mama prayed for nearly ten years for Boaz. You know—the provider, protector, *the one* who loves you, warts and all, otherwise known as Prince Charming.

My Prince Charming didn't come with directions. He came with a mindset all his own! Even so, he was the first man in my life who didn't try to *control* me. He loved my sassiness, free spirit, and senseless zaniness for life, and he appreciated the deep faith God had planted within my heart and my attempt at being obedient to Christ.

My attempt in the obedience department, however, didn't translate into obedience or submissiveness to Charming. Apparently, that's a learned skill absorbed after the initial shock 'n' awe of marriage!

It was odd that he and I could sit for hours tallying the

checkbook and arguing about money and come up empty-handed every time. Literally! Why couldn't he just let go and let me handle it? An unsolved mystery! He knew I could take care of business. Turning it over to me would solve all our quarreling. Give that checkbook up, Buck-o!

Another issue—who was in the driver's seat on long trips? Or even a trip to town and back? Naturally, after being a single mama for years, I was used to driving *and* doing checkbooks!

One day it occurred to me—yikes—I had a control nut in my bed!

I knew God hadn't made a mistake in bringing our marriage together, so I asked, "What's up, Lord? If this is going to work, somebody's got to give up control."

Then boom! God said, "You'll never have total control until you give *Me* total control." Ouch. *You mean I'm the one who's to surrender, Lord?* Well, butter my biscuit!

When we Jezebel brides surrender our control to Mr. Charming—a husband who heeds God's Word and loves us like Christ loves the Church—we may find that we live happily ever after. I did!

Sweet surrendering and submitting,

Candy A. Westbrook

≈29≈

OBSESSED WITH WORDS

Dear Obsessed with Words,

I can identify with your situation, because I also have said things and not realized how my words came across until later—much later. One instance quickly comes to mind.

It seems that throughout most of my marriage, my husband and I haven't quite stayed on the same page when it came to getting things done around the house. I have to admit, the meanings of the words *you* and *we* are a bit elusive. When asking your new friend to come over for dessert, does the phrase, "Would you like to come over for cake tomorrow night?" mean for her to come, her and her husband, or her, her husband, and her six children? That's the reason in the south we default to *you* (singular) and *y'all* (plural).

The word *we* presents much the same problem. Whenever I mentioned that we needed to mow the yard, how could he miss that I meant he needed to mow it?

After all, we only own one mower. Did he think we would walk hand-in-hand and use our other hand to hold the mower handle? Or when I said we needed to redecorate the den, did he not understand that I would decide what would be changed and most likely he would do the majority of the work?

Being a problem-solving woman, especially of communication problems, I came up with a new language for us. There would be *me-we* for things I would do, *you-we* for things he would handle, and *we-we* for things to be done together, as in "We need to go out for ice cream."

Since implementing this system, misunderstandings regarding who does what rarely occur between us. We wanted to help others possibly experiencing similar troubles, so we shared our process with several friends. We did not understand their bemused expressions. Having never had children and not being experts in preschool language, it wasn't until a young family visited us one weekend and we shared our unique insights with them that we understood—the difference is in the *e*.

No longer do we publicly share *me-we*, *you-we*, or *we-we* for fear some child will think we need to go potty.

Seriously—that's not what I meant,

Lynn Nester

≈30≈

BRAKE LIGHT WATCHER

Dear Brake Light Watcher,

Anyone who travels in Atlanta can relate to our traffic woes. Drivers consistently demonstrate a "me-first" attitude once they commence their commute.

The aggravation starts when a driver is cut off, causing horns to honk and other drivers to swerve to miss the ensuing argument between the angry drivers. It's like a boxing match where cars replace fists.

My travel begins on north I-75. As I merge onto the interstate, I join with other cars and lots of semi-tractor trailers. The radio alerts everyone to major mishaps, but most days I pass one or two fender benders never mentioned on the radio. Cars bob and weave then rush to a standstill. Brake lights flash. I'm on and off the brakes for miles as I merge with I-575 traffic and travel through Marietta.

The overhead sign announces 29-31 minutes for the ten-mile drive to the intersection with Delk Road. Farther down the road, I make my way onto I-285 traveling east. On the highway sign I frequently read, "West 55+ mph" and "East 23 mph." I look ahead and face another sea of bright red brake lights and several more miles of stop and go traffic that I must endure before I arrive at my workplace.

How do I survive such an ordeal? I've learned to relax and take my time when staring at brake lights for hours on end. I use my time to listen to inspirational books on CD or to the Christian radio station, 104.7 "The Fish." Sometimes I make hands-free telephone calls or use the confined time to pray, especially for those in the accidents I pass. It doesn't do any good for me to get angry. Changing my thoughts of dread to gratitude has made this daily trip tolerable. And when I arrive at work, I thank the Lord that I haven't been in an accident and that I have made it to work, even when I'm late.

Since you're a fellow brake light watcher, hopefully you've found avenues to make the best of your commute. It's all about perspective.

Changed perspective,

Sue Schultz

≈31≈

DEPRESSION ADDICT

Dear Depression Addict,

I don't like to talk about the "out of control" periods in my life. Do you also smile and pretend everything is fine when you feel you may not make it through the day?

Life has brought me to the edge of insanity more than once. I wallowed in depression, whined and lied about it, and threw a private pity-party. Those things didn't make the problems go away.

When depression descends, we lose control and feel all alone. As you know, it's not just feeling sad or being unhappy with life's circumstances. Depression is an all-encompassing cloud of darkness that zaps your desire to live. It sucks the life out of you and leaves you whimpering in defeat.

Friends, family members, and church members tend to avoid you. After all, you're no fun to be around. They may judge your weakness, say you're depressed because of sins you've committed, and suggest you should smile and not talk about it.

My release from depression's grip happened only when I hit the bottom of the dark pit, fell on my face before God, and accepted His healing. He lifted me up because I couldn't do it myself. To block further attack, I prepared through prayer and Scripture. Before that worked, though, I had to declare that I *wanted* to overcome depression. Self-pity feels so good sometimes.

One effective way I battle depression is by reaching out to others who need help. Depression is a selfish condition that seduces you and causes you to concentrate solely on yourself and your personal misery. When you look beyond yourself, you're halfway to victory. When I reach out, people I've never met face-to-face read about my journey on Facebook or blogs and approach me. They tell me their stories. I listen, without judgment. We pray; we share cyber tears. Their suffering is validated. I challenge them to stand up, denounce depression, and battle with determination.

Are you crushed by depression? There is hope. If someone you know is clinging to the edge of a precipice, take their hand and walk alongside them toward hope and help.

No longer addicted,

Karen Nolan Bell

≈32≈

REMOTE CONTROL ROULETTER

Dear Remote Control Rouletter,

Since the advent of satellite dishes and cable TV, which provide hundreds of options for visual entertainment, the single most revolutionary advance in television technology isn't the plasma screen, High Definition, or 3D TVs. It's the remote control. No need to leave the comfort of your favorite spot to change the station. The push of a button or two starts the channel guide spinning like a roulette wheel. Where will your little ball land?

This handy device also addresses one of television viewers' most perplexing problems. How do we deal with those aggravating commercials? The moment one appears I can jump to another station and avoid it like the plague. In addition, I can watch several things at once: news, sports, sitcoms, and so forth. I'm a commercial free multitasker!

My proficiency developed into an art form. I flipped from program to program with lightning speed.

Unfortunately, not everyone shared my enthusiasm for remote control roulette. No fan of advertisements, my better half grew tired of the constant disruption of his favorite show. I'm not as adept as I'd like to believe. On several occasions I returned to the original broadcast to find it already in progress. Not good. A quiet evening of relaxation took on the frenzied atmosphere of a casino. Something had to change.

The solution was simple. When possible we record the programs we like. The ability to fast forward through the commercials allows more time to view actual content. If we wish to switch to live programming, we hit the pause button and pick back up later wherever we left off.

Our TV time is now serene and peaceful. My better half is so relaxed he falls asleep, confident that he won't miss anything. I still control the remote but with a more deliberate, sophisticated approach. Now we're both winners.

Maybe you suffer from remote control roulette and drive family and friends to distraction. A DVR or digital video recorder is your answer. Eliminate commercials, switch channels, and you won't miss a moment of your favorite shows. When on your own, get your game on and spin the channel guide to your heart's content. Anyway you look at it, everyone wins.

Stationary for the moment,

Mary Agrusa

≈33≈

TOO MUCH PRIDE

Dear Too Much Pride,

Let me tell you about one day when I should have known better than to do what I did.

When you take your pantyhose off the line in the morning and one foot is facing forward and the other is facing backwards, you *know* it's going to be a bad day.

I didn't expect a bad day as a new employee on the sales floor in Wood Valley at Rich's Cumberland store—the shopping mecca of Cobb County. I was decked out in a new melon-colored pantsuit with a melon-striped top under my jacket and, very likely, melon-colored sandals to match. (Nowadays, I would call that *overkill!*) Also in those days, if we wanted to look good, we *had* to have our hair done in a piled up-do that my children called a "high-up hairdo." I could hardly enter my car without leaning.

I'm sure I walked with a lilt in my step that day, thinking I looked so good. Today, I wouldn't be caught dead in such a bright get-up. Surely I have better taste now!

Nature called, and I decided to make the shorter trip across the mall atrium to go to Macy's ladies' room instead of to the ladies' room at Rich's. I prided myself on my *everything-new*, *everything-matching* pantsuit and, no doubt, those matching sandals. I thought I really looked awesome.

Macy's had mirrored posts every few feet along the pathway. *What a great decorating idea!* I thought. I likely admired myself in every post I passed on the way back to Rich's ... until I spotted about an arm's length of toilet paper hanging from the back of my jacket and gently floating in the breeze. I looked around to see if anyone was looking and quickly jerked that embarrassing paper from behind me. I was as red-faced as my matching suit!

As you know, pride goeth before a fall, and my goeth was about to fall that day.

Still embarrassed,

June Parks

≈34≈

STASHER

Dear Stasher,

What a pleasure it is to encounter people like me who hold on to their possessions for special occasions. I find comfort knowing we coexist as soul mates. No need to fret, we don't stockpile like hoarders. Often, we save items because we lack the finances for our everyday needs. So we stash things away to make sure they are available for important events. Doesn't it feel good to pull out impressive objects for those special times? Yet we both know those events rarely occur.

One afternoon while preparing dinner, I asked my daughter to fill our plates. Entering the kitchen, I found her pulling the good dishes from the cabinet.

"No! We only use the china when company comes."

"Mom, I thought we could use it this one time."

"Maybe the next time," I said

Shaking her head, my daughter put the exquisite dishes back.

When I think about that incident, I can't help but laugh. In reality, when company eventually visited, I used paper plates to avoid washing the dishes!

Can you keep a secret? Not only did I reserve the china for special occasions, but the plush bath towels were also stored only for guests while my children and I used the worn ones. Let's not forget the exclusive perfumes that I saved for those rare nights on the town. I'm sorry to say, they sometimes turned rancid before I could use half of them. Even the lobster developed freezer burn after months of waiting for that fancy dinner.

Instead of storing our belongings for a day that may never come, why don't we make *today* special. God wants us to place our trust only in Him. He recognizes our struggles, and we can depend on His promises to supply all of our needs. Let's learn to live in the present without worry about tomorrow and to enjoy the blessings and provisions bestowed upon us this day.

Dining on china,

Vanessa Fortenberry

≈35≈

WORKER BEE

Dear Worker Bee,

Corporate America. It has an orchestra all its own. The chime of a new message or email, the ringing of a phone, keyboards tapping—all are music to my ears. Some of us thrive in the constant busyness of a demanding career. The more pressure, the better we perform. It's the perfect scenario for competing against ourselves. We live for the satisfaction of wrapping up a project or seeing results from our contributed expertise.

Before the invention of the wheel, I wrote for live television. I'd never known such tight deadlines. Pulling a show together could quickly unravel, causing pandemonium in the scramble to land upright. Stories often fell apart in nanoseconds. The job was not for the faint of heart and demanded sacrifices.

My office was directly outside of the newsroom. Colleagues were stunned that I actually wanted it, as it had sat vacant for months. Crews ran in and out as stories

73

broke and voices escalated. I thrived on the synergy. My work transferred to home where I'd interview guests late into the night. It suited me perfectly.

But then marriage and family arrived, challenging my earlier demands. Still wired the same, I had new tasks needing a reconfiguration of my equipment. Increasing years brought new challenges, but with them came wisdom and an overhaul in values. Suddenly, my children's milestones and grandchildren's arrival rearranged the playing field.

This change in priorities helped me live in a healthier way. No deathbed hospital patient has ever said, "I wish I'd spent more time at the office." I've learned that he who burns the candle at both ends self-extinguishes. Our week intentionally contains a Sabbath, and our nightly Sabbath is sleep. These are set times to rejuvenate our worn bodies and souls.

What about our loved ones? How long should they have to wait for us to realize their value? We've only got one lifetime to fill their treasure chests with loving memories.

Perhaps it's time to inventory our priorities. Take the trip. Attend the reunion. Worship in church. It's fine to buzz with excitement, but perhaps we should consider buzzing longer at our home's hive.

Enjoying my honey,

Susan M. Watkins

≈36≈

WANNABE WORKOUT WOMAN

Dear Wannabe Workout Woman,

I admit it. I'm addicted to exercise classes and have been for over thirty years, but it hasn't always been that way. When I first started, I felt nervous, out of place. I had to force myself to go. Maybe you feel the same way and it has kept you from signing up. For me, curiosity won out. I had to discover why so many people loved to go and why they talked about all the benefits of working out.

While exercising, I observed ten different types who attend workout classes. They came in an array of shapes and sizes.

1. **The Over-the-Topper:** An overachiever who does every routine to her utmost ability, full throttle.

2. **The Minimalist:** Does the least she can get by with and barely breaks a sweat.

3. **The Clapper:** Loves to add claps or snaps to routines whenever possible.

4. **The Dance to Your Own Beater:** A rebel at heart, she's convinced that her individual moves are much better than the instructor's.

5. **The Front Rower:** Gets disgruntled if there's no room for her up front and hates when the instructor asks her to change places.

6. **The Back Rower:** Remains determined to stay in the back and hates to be asked to move even more than the Front Rower.

7. **The Mojoer:** Has found her rhythm and groove and relishes the fact that she has a place to express it on a regular basis.

8. **The Aerobically Challenged:** Has never found her rhythm and stays one step behind for the entire hour.

9. **The Token Male:** A real man—brave and rarely spotted in class.

10. **The Die Harder:** Attends class even though she is sick, injured, or can barely move because of an especially hard workout the day before.

So, find your exercise personality and go shake a leg! I promise—you'll never regret it, and your mind, body, and soul will thank you.

Waiting for you in class,

Susan Browning Schulz

PART 3

FINANCIALLY CHALLENGED

And my God will meet all your needs according to his
glorious riches in Christ Jesus.
—Philippians 4:19

≈37≈

CLEARANCE RACK RAIDER

Dear Clearance Rack Raider,

Our thriftiness gives us a common bond. While others shop as a pastime, we do it out of necessity. Like me, you've probably bought a jacket during an end of season markdown. Maybe you've purchased jeans from a thrift store or plucked clothing from a closet of hand-me-downs.

That's okay. We all experience lean times and want to look special—even through our struggles.

Several years ago, I sported one of my bargains. Clothed in a jacket that put Pepto-Bismol-pink on the color wheel, my confidence soared. I beamed in several directions. Hoping for a brief appearance on the Jumbotron, I chose a conspicuous seat near the front.

I craved compliments, photographs, and fanfare. But cameras didn't flash. After clearing my throat several times, I garnered no attention. My pleasant greetings failed to arouse double takes. After all, I was at church, not an NBA game.

As the youth choir began a popular selection, I leapt from the pew. Belting out the tune, I clapped my hands and swayed to the music. My new pink jacket moved in sync. I felt womanly.

A gentle tap on my shoulder interrupted me. "Mom," my daughter whispered, "*your tag!*"

Embarrassed, I hastened to the pew. I snatched off the redlined clearance tag and removed a clear pouch containing an extra hot pink button. The unsightly duo had rocked under my arm and clanked against my side the entire time.

Minutes later, a woman leaned toward me. "I love your *new* jacket."

"You noticed," I murmured.

Nodding vigorously, the woman admitted, "I've done the same thing, too." Her warm smile offered reassurance.

Whether dust or dollars line our pockets, God loves us equally. It's comforting to know that He provides the best wardrobe accessories free of charge. We can always wear a smile; it never goes out of season. Squared shoulders exude confidence. Lifting our chins, we have greater visibility and appear more approachable. And let's not forget the most important fashion tip: tag is a childhood game—not something we wear to broadcast our bargains.

Pretty embarrassed in pink,

Cherise Bopape

≈38≈

SURVIVOR

Dear Survivor,

Delightful autumn colors and sunshine lifted my spirits as I walked into work that Monday morning. Then my boss called me aside, informing me that my position had been closed. I looked out the window; the sun still shone, but I wondered why. Stunned with the news, I felt too numb for coherent thought, let alone a decent appeal. Twenty-three years earlier I had jokingly told my wife, "This is temporary." Now I felt breathless, as if punched in the stomach. Many of my friends and acquaintances consoled me with the adage, "When one door closes, another opens," but at the time I failed to fully understand.

Before I lost my job, I remember my golfing partner asking me, as I rounded the ninth hole, what I did for a living. I was taken aback, at a loss for words. To some extent I lacked a clear purpose. As much as I loved my job, I enjoyed writing novels, too. God changed my focus in November 2012. I walked out of work with my head held high, though my heart was broken. The next morning I awoke with a mission. I had a story to write, another one to edit, and yet another one to promote. I had a reason to live.

Within a few days, a man hired me as a freelance writer for his father's memoir. Every day brought new and exciting writing opportunities. I believe God has called me to write. It's a unique ministry, one that many people aspire to, yet in which few succeed. The admonition from a friend to "keep writing" propels me forward. No longer do I suffer from an identity crisis, for I have found a new calling. I am a literary missionary.

So be encouraged; there is a reason to live; there is something useful for you to do. Keep pursuing your dreams. Don't give up, but keep going.

Still surviving and thriving,

Bryan M. Powell

≈39≈

PEDAL PUSHER

Some debts are fun when you are acquiring them, but none are fun when you set about retiring them.

–Ogden Nash

Dear Pedal Pusher,

My husband and I lived the American dream. Or maybe I should call it a nightmare. Our combined student loans, a business loan, and multiple credit card debts prompted a financial planner to exclaim, "I've never seen two people with so much debt!" Not very comforting to hear from a man who makes his living helping others put their financial ducks in a row.

The sheer embarrassment from that comment, along with the fact that we spoke to our creditors more than to our family members, inspired us to embark on a debt-free journey. I knew it would be a trip. I was expecting the high-speed rail to financial freedom. What I've experienced has been more like a meandering bike ride.

One warm Easter afternoon, I cycled the Silver Comet Trail with my daughter Hope. She pedaled with all her might. Her long, brown hair tossed in the breeze. I followed her lead. Then she slowed to a coast, and I did, too. When her leg muscles and lungs recovered, she cranked her pedals, gained momentum, hit her peak speed, and then slowed again. We repeated this pattern several times. I then told my daughter, "Whew! I'm worn out. You can keep that up if you want, but I'm pedaling at a constant speed." She maintained her cycling strategy, but with my steady pace, I crossed the finish line first.

Our debt-free plan, or lack of one, was much like that bike ride. With gusto, my husband and I started the journey to good stewardship. We pedaled vigorously toward our goal. We sacrificed and made progress. Then we relaxed and coasted for a while. Our debt-free dream kept eluding us.

Then we changed course and developed a steady pay-off plan. With patience and faithful devotion to that plan, we could finally see the finish line to financial freedom. We've learned that you'll make the greatest strides pedaling to prosperity by keeping a constant speed. See you at the finish line!

Steady as she goes,

Theresa Anderson

≈40≈

FINANCIALLY STRAPPED

Dear Financially Strapped,

In 1993, I bought a dealership loaner car at a significant discount. Then I got a promotion which included use of a company vehicle. No problem, I thought, *just sell the '92 Prism.*

But my Toyota Corolla look-alike didn't sell over the next eight months, and payroll deductions for using the company vehicle were steeper than planned.

After six months I moved the Prism, which was with my family in central New York, to my Long Island residence, hopeful for a better market. Advertising in the local weekly *Auto Trader* and parking so commuters could see the "For Sale" signs still failed to generate any bona fide offers. Saddled with two car payments, I worried more and more about my financial situation. Could a job promotion lead to financial downturn?

The situation worsened. I received a 30-day warning from property management: "Remove the car from the premises or it will be towed to the police impound."

Worry turned to panic. I sought out my Bible study group and asked them to pray that my car would sell. I also suggested they ask their friends if someone needed a midsized car with low mileage.

A couple contacted me to see the car and discuss the asking price. Their son was headed for college soon and needed transportation. My goal was to have enough cash to pay off the loan, plus a small amount to ease the financial hurdles I faced.

Although the car was over their budget, what relief I felt when the couple agreed to buy it. Their generosity and kindness released me from the dread of looming financial disaster. Only one week had remained to close the deal before my credit was ruined. In addition, my company's high standards for their field representatives would have also jeopardized my job.

From this experience I learned that God is never too early or too late when circumstances are beyond *our* control. While not all trials have such a happy ending, God works through His people as we trust Him.

Free from Prism prison,

Laura Garron Havens

≈41≈

BARELY MAKING IT

Dear Barely Making It,

I know we all have times when we need a little more money to make it to payday. I've been there more times than I can count. But I've also had times when a little more wasn't enough.

A few years ago at Thanksgiving, my husband's job ended. With optimism, I decorated the Christmas tree with treasured ornaments and left it up until a new job justified gift-giving. I had no idea that tree would sit there for eighteen months!

An economic depression in my husband's industry eventually took all of our savings and curtailed any extras. I began studying the book of Job as menus tightened, doctor visits disappeared, and life-sustaining medicine bottles sat empty.

Our dignity took a beating as we begged for assistance for utilities and used Medicare and food stamps. We stood in long lines at churches to get only ten or twenty dollars to help pay our utilities and wondered why we bothered.

Soon, demanding creditors called every day. Then our car was repossessed, my son had to enroll in public school his senior year, and a foreclosure notice arrived. I stared bitterly at our forlorn Christmas tree. As I stared, it began slowly leaning, then crashed to the floor, carrying with it all our beautiful decorations. God's love for me seemed to shatter as well, and I wanted to give up. Instead, I fell on my knees and gave Him control—over everything.

Changes began. The Christian school called and told me someone had paid my son's tuition. Medicare provided my medications. We still had my decrepit little car and we still had each other.

Then my husband found a job right before my son's graduation. Even though we lost our house and many of our possessions, the Lord timed it so we had a place to live until moving day.

God doesn't promise we won't struggle—and struggles aren't always someone's fault. But He proved to me that He is enough. I now look back on that time and see that He provided what was necessary. And yes, God loves us, even when we doubt.

Always enough,

Karen Nolan Bell

≈42≈

FEELING BROKE

Dear Feeling Broke,

The jangle of the telephone interrupted my newspaper reading. At this time of night? It was 11 p.m. "Hello, Grandma," my granddaughter Melissa brightly greeted me.

At the University of Georgia, she had a report due the next day and had forgotten it until a friend asked if her paper was ready. She had to quiz someone over 60 and knew precisely who to interview. She calls me her most unforgettable character.

We talked until 2 a.m. as I reminisced about my life. When Melissa asked what my favorite age was, I had to think a few minutes. Then I decided it was when my four kids were all stairsteps ranging from ages two to eight.

Another question brought a quick answer with many reflections afterwards. She asked, "As an older person, what would you change?"

The answer popped out of my mouth "I would have saved more money." I've hit that dreaded fixed income stage, which means *exactly* what it says. The pay is fixed, but expenses are not. When the dollars give out after paying bills, it's all gone. You have to make the money stretch to afford to eat. Through the years I had spent money on my family, then realized later the value of saving.

Since I was raised frugally, I'm not so disappointed now. When you're old, you take forward steps, and if you're happy and *smart*, you smile. That broke condition won't change, but it won't bother you easily. Most people I know are in the same boat; it's a common feeling.

After disclosing my thoughts and revisiting many life experiences, I felt so much closer to my precious Melissa. Later she told me she received a grade of 95 on her paper. As we sat at lunch the next week, I smugly told Melissa I thought her excellent score was due to the subject matter. She smiled and agreed!

Broke but Blessed Grandmother,

June Parks

≈43≈

SOLO PARENT

Dear Solo Parent,

I was labeled by the IRS as "Single, Head of Household" through separation and divorce. My discretionary spending drastically changed. Designer clothes and weekly visits to Charles of Atlantic City for that perfect look vanished. During the 1970s gas rationing, it hurt to fuel my car. I mapped the shortest route to complete errands before leaving home.

On weekdays my toddler needed a babysitter. Expenses for food, clothing, and rent depleted my cash flow. As the judge had recently indicated, child support payments made welfare seem appealing.

When caring friends would question how I was making it, "on a wing and a prayer" was my honest response. I often continued ... "and with a little help from my friends." I have come to cherish those years of financial discipline.

I remember the quality, joy-filled times together with

my daughter. We rode bikes, camped, and roller-skated. We fed ducks at lakes, tossed balls, and played board games. In the summertime, we went to the beach and bought ice cream from the vendor there. Carrying the heavy ice chest on his shoulders, he would trudge through the sand to us as we basked in the sun. When the sea breeze cooled, we sauntered down the boardwalk looking for intriguing shops.

My daughter Debbie began her lifelong hobby of singing by joining junior choir at the same church where I served as her Bible study teacher. When she was ten, a job transfer took us to Syracuse, New York, where we continued to make forever friends through church social networking. Our outdoor recreation now included snow and mountain fun.

As the years flew by, Debbie grew into an awesome teenager who tested my mom skills. We survived in spite of our generational gap and watched the doors open for her to enter college.

Single parenting has its challenges. However, as we bring our financial situation under control, life's other problems can be handled with confidence and a loving attitude. We are never stuck in our present predicament. We can transform tough times by tackling our adverse circumstances "on a wing and a prayer."

Divorced but not down and out,

Laura Garron Havens

≈44≈

PENNILESS PERFECTIONIST

Dear Penniless Perfectionist,

Please tell me you love plastic containers, sticky labels, and fancy file folders as much as I do. I must admit—my heart pounds with excitement when I delay writing articles to categorize paper clips, stacks of paper, and electronic in-boxes. However, it doesn't stop there. I need, yes NEED, everything in my life to be perfect before I can sit down and be creative. My main reason for an empty bank account is my need for organization

Unfortunately, when I attempt to write, dust bunnies multiply like the tribbles from Star Trek until they are all I can see. Dirty dishes like ancient ruins pile up on the kitchen counters. Skyscrapers of papers threaten to fall on me. They all scream for my attention. When I heed their cry, my computer screen remains blank. I fool myself into believing I am too busy to write. Is your income flow stymied by similar distractions?

Everything changed when my failing health prevented

me from chasing the bunnies, doing the laundry regularly, or controlling the stacks of dishes. So my excuses altered as well. Instead of blaming my lack of productivity on being orderly, I blamed it on my *inability* to organize. As I stared at the spider dangling in front of my monitor, I lamented my low achievement. "If only," I sighed.

While wallowing in a slough of self-pity, I had an epiphany. I realized that my life will never be perfect. Therefore, my creative writing submissions must emerge from the imperfection. God actually proves His perfection and ownership of our work by creating beauty from our stumbling efforts.

Today I sit at my computer surrounded by a mess equal to a college professor's office on retirement day. The dust bunnies and spiders fill in the spaces between heaps and piles. However, I am creating from my heart and allowing God to transform it for me. Hopefully that means a check in the mail, too. I must never forget that if I do my job, He will provide the finances.

Content with the mess,

Karen Nolan Bell

≈45≈

STRETCHED TO THE BREAKING POINT

Dear Stretched to the Breaking Point,

Are your finances stretched so thin you need a magnifying glass to find them? Does a trip to the mall leave you frustrated and angry? If so, you're not alone but in good company.

People worldwide have been impacted by the global financial crisis. In some cases, poor money management is the problem, but not always. Hard working, responsible individuals face difficult circumstances due to job loss, health problems, investment reversals, or business failures. Several years ago, my husband and I found something that helped us face financial headwinds and stay aloft.

Early in our marriage, my husband decided that all credit card balances would be paid off each month. I was aghast—my shopping wings were clipped. When my instant gratification crash-landed, shopping wasn't fun anymore. Everyone else was buying up a storm except me and my grounded credit cards. For years I resented the tethers on our spending. Then I learned a little secret.

I discovered the benefits of using OPM (Other People's Money). At that time checking accounts paid interest. When I used my credit cards, my funds sat in the bank and collected interest. No charges and fees were assessed when I paid in full. I used the credit card company's cash as a short term interest-free loan. Sale items now really were bargains.

When the cash back bonus was instituted, I profited even more. I wasn't charged for the money I borrowed, and I was rewarded for using someone else's funds and not mine. I got paid to shop sensibly.

Although no one enjoys tight financial times, they can teach us to make wiser money management decisions. Necessity *is* the mother of invention. Our tight spot can lead us to innovative ideas that broaden our horizons and fatten our wallets, such as using OPM. Let's not succumb to despair; it curtails creativity. Let's keep our eyes open for unusual opportunities from unexpected sources and courageously step into these new adventures as they appear.

Snapping back into financial shape,

Mary Agrusa

≈46≈

WINNER WANNABE

Dear Winner Wannabe,

How many times have you won the lottery? If you are like me, the answer is never. As a matter of personal conviction, I've never played the lottery. But, ask me how many times I've filled out a Home Depot survey hoping to win five thousand dollars, or pulled off the scratch and win sticker from a soft drink can and scratched it wildly, or sat with crossed fingers, hoping my initials BP19305 would appear on the Wheel of Fortune proclaiming me the winner of five thousand dollars. Sadly, I have to confess I have done it many times. So I ask myself, "Why?" Do I actually think my life would be better if I won? It would certainly help my checkbook, but as far as improving the person I am, five thousand dollars would not make that much difference.

Actually, I consider myself already a winner. I can stand, walk, run if I choose to, and enjoy food and other pleasures of life. I can see, hear, smell, taste, touch, breathe

God's clear air every morning, and pillow my head at night without fear. I have a faithful wife, loving children and grandchildren, and devoted friends who care about my well-being.

Yes, my heart has been broken. I know the searing pain of betrayal, the disappointment of financial setbacks, and the anguish of failing health, but I choose to be thankful for what I have, and not dwell on what I've lost. I daily practice an attitude of gratitude.

You may not have the same blessings as mine. You may have already lost some of the benefits of life, but you can still consider yourself a winner. As a Christian, you already have heaven as your home, the Word of God as your guide, and the presence of God as your constant companion. With blessings like these, you are a winner.

Always a winner,

Bryan M. Powell

≈47≈

CHICKEN KING GENERAL MANAGER

Dear Chicken King General Manager,

I wish to thank the staff of the East Point Chicken King Restaurant for allowing me to participate in the taste test for your new barbeque recipes. I am earnest when I say that your new product survey was a true lifesaver.

My mother and I had been experiencing a run of bad luck when we stopped at your restaurant. We had scratched together enough loose change to indulge in the purchase of a small drumstick combo. Payday was several weeks away, and it was hard to face another supper of pinto beans or ketchup soup. (This soup consists of ketchup squeezed from fast food condiment packets into hot water.)

Before we could approach the front counter to place an order, we were greeted by a courteous employee who asked if we had a few minutes to participate in a taste test. I would have agreed to taste anything, even if it had been a

99

piece of cardboard dipped in hot sauce.

Imagine our surprise when two pieces of chicken and two side items were set before each of us. We were even provided soft drinks! Since it was a rainy night with few customers in the store, the employee returned to request we give our opinions of three more flavors. A large to-go box was provided for our uneaten food, along with a refill of our soft drinks.

Your staff treated us like royalty at a time when I felt like my opinion, much less my very existence, didn't matter. Though months passed before our fortunes significantly improved, the gloom lifted some that night. Also, I developed a keen appreciation for companies that have shown us a kindness, no matter how small.

Saying goodbye to ketchup soup,

Cheryl Anderson Davis

P.S. Although I truly enjoyed all four flavors, please make sure my preferred honey recipe continues to be served in all your restaurants!

≈48≈

CHALLENGED WIDOW

Dear Challenged Widow,

At the tender age of eight, I lost my superhero dad to cancer. That same year, Mom was diagnosed with multiple sclerosis. She determined to keep all five daughters in her heart and home with monthly $250 welfare checks.

However, three years later we lost our eleven-room farmhouse in a rural community of South Jersey. It was sad saying good-bye to friends and the Garron homestead on 75 acres of beautiful trees, creeks, and fields where deer grazed. Those childhood years are now precious memories. We eventually moved into a modern brick government project in a prestigious Atlantic City suburb.

Despite our limited income, we experienced a teeming social life. We spent summers not as tourists on this coastal island, but as full time residents. We body surfed in the ocean, strolled the full length of the boardwalk, and people-watched. I even danced on Dick Clark's famous American Bandstand on the Steel Pier, later demolished by a northeaster storm.

Mom shaped us into a do-it-yourself family, and thanks to our tender loving care, furniture and household belongings exceeded their normal life expectancy. She found an in-home freezer meal plan that kept us well fed and arranged for school programs that provided gently worn clothing and hot lunches. But I skipped lunch in high school, aware of the stigma attached to the tickets used only by students on welfare.

Stretching every penny, Mom always eked out enough money for special treats. The extravagance we girls remember most was our weekly donuts from Atlantic Donuts mobile bakery. Though the baker carefully placed the goodies in a box, it emptied soon. Before our move, we had relished farm treats of cold watermelon and occasional 5-cent drinks or ice cream cones if we walked the two miles to the soda fountain.

Through the years, my mother always counted her blessings before her problems. Although you may be a widowed mother with meager worldly assets and little money, pray for the grace to be content. When your children see your grateful spirit, they won't miss what they don't have. Your love and encouragement trumps anything this world can offer them.

Blessed through poverty,

Laura Garron Havens

≈49≈

TAPPED-OUT PARENT

Dear Tapped-Out Parent,

Does it seem as though cash drains continuously from your pockets and pocketbooks with the mounting cost of living? Money's scarce, especially since your children were born. Visions of dollars taking wing and sounds of cash register bells haunt you!

From cradle to college, our must-have lists for children include cribs, dressers, diapers, food, clothes, toys, books, bedroom furniture, shoes, school supplies, and tuition. It's a list that grows with them. How can families afford it?

For my husband and me, marriage provided the love of a spouse as well as the arduous feat of furnishing a home on a tight budget. Ah, fulfilling the dream of owning a home and literally living on the floor! Since we had little money, we looked for furniture bargains while eating rice and beans. An old cupboard with table and chairs fit our breakfast nook, and two-by-four planks fashioned into living room furniture served our needs.

Just as we began to make ends meet, I became pregnant with our first child. Baby essentials demanded our attention and more remarkable finds surfaced, like a used $25 crib needing repair and unfinished furniture doubling as a dresser and changing table. Immediately we worked on our new possessions and happily ate our rice and beans. Before long, our daughter arrived on the scene and the only place to put her was in my husband's office. Juggling their varied schedules challenged us all.

Life sped by and suddenly we needed two incomes to pay for college. Because all our money went to our children's education, we continued eating rice and beans. Can you imagine the look on our faces when one night our children told us about grilling steaks for supper with their friends? Oh, the joys of parenthood!

Children grow up fast and eventually leave home. They cost tons of money and time, but are worth every penny and minute. Enjoy them and make wise decisions as you sacrifice for them. From cradle to college, raising children is a priceless endeavor.

Realizing benefits,

Deborah Crawford

≈50≈

PENNY PINCHER

Dear Penny Pincher,

Not many people remember what happened five decades ago, but my memories are profound and deep-seated. The good times stay with me.

I remember one Mother's Day when my sister and I were eight and ten years old. Daddy always waited until the last minute to buy gifts. Maybe he didn't know until the end of the week how much he could spend. Daddy was generous, but he just didn't earn enough to be a big spender.

We didn't begin shopping for Mom until the big day, and only *after* church. As we walked into our neighboring florist shop, the distinctive aroma of all those flowers enveloped us. The three of us circled the room and immediately disagreed about our gift for Mom.

Right there on the showroom floor, a gorgeous basket garden bursting with color caught our attention. We loved it! Betty and I decided on that one, but Daddy's face told us that the price tag did not match the money in his wallet. We were disappointed and begged Daddy to buy that beautiful one anyway.

It seemed like forever until Betty and I could finally agree to a small dish garden. The florist knew us, so she added a couple of blooms and a pretty bow on the gift, but it just couldn't compare with the gorgeous basket garden.

Mother, who hadn't seen the magnificent basket, exclaimed in delight at her gift. Betty and I learned that sometimes the biggest and best gift won't fit the budget. If you can't afford it, just don't buy it. The most valuable gift is given from the heart.

Still penny-pinching,

June Parks

≈51≈

FINANCIALLY CHALLENGED

Dear Financially Challenged,

Managing money on a tiny budget is tough. I've had to do it.

Years ago my husband changed jobs. His new benefit package offered great perks, but for several months we would have a shortfall in our budget. In three months he would get another raise that would solve the problem. If we could sell a car, we could use that money until he was paid more.

I'd never sold anything and didn't know where to start. So I looked at our income and thought about where I could cut back. I decided I would hold back giving to the church until the crunch was over. The moment I chose that path, I felt guilty. Would it please God to take money intended for His glory and use it for my own comfort? So I told God I wouldn't use the money we allocated for church.

But the car presented a problem. I hate selling

107

anything, and my heart pounded with the tension. I reminded myself of the many missionaries who all proclaimed that God provided. Scripture also recounts stories, like the manna God gave when the Israelites had no food. That night we had Bible study at church, and I shared that we had to sell a car. Several people asked questions, and then we prayed. After the meeting, a man came up and said he and his wife needed a car and wanted to buy it. My mouth fell open. I guess I thought we'd have to list it in the paper and offer test drives. The couple had not been married long, and my first thought was that they were being nice. Instead, they bought the car. I was so amazed that it worked out. I'd never lived through a situation where God provided so clearly. He did it, even though I wasn't a missionary.

I learned a lesson. From that point on, I made up my mind to trust God. He's always provided, and He will do the same for you.

Trusting God for manna from heaven,

Cynthia L. Simmons

≈52≈

LIQUIDATING

Dear Liquidating,

I've heard the song. You worked all your life and this is all you have to show for it. You spent a career burning the midnight oil only to see your earnings go up in smoke. Equity's gone. Retirement account drained. Savings depleted. Credit cards maxed. Robbing Peter to pay Paul has become an art form. It's easy to feel so overwhelmed you can't see any way out of your current predicament; however, closed doors give way to open windows.

Like most everyone, I've watched my home's equity evaporate like water drops on a hot griddle. Working, saving, sacrificing, and suddenly it's gone. You find yourself starting from scratch. I've had jobs vanish or, after being offered, never materialize. I've seen credit card debt inch higher while wondering how to retain my home. I've spent time in food pantries and explored discharge options. Once, during a brittle stretch, someone asked if I dated. I replied, "Yes, I liquidate." It may feel like you're in a race to the bottom, but maybe you've got some buried treasure in your abilities that warrants evaluation.

The best news is realizing you're not in this struggle alone. God cares for His people. Others have wrestled the same issues and survived. Things often resolve differently than expected, but it's the resolution that demands focus. Maybe it's time to reinvent yourself or open that business you've always dreamed of owning. To rid yourself of preconceived ideas sometimes unlocks that stubborn door. Explore new options. This dry season may be just what you need to switch careers. Opportunities are often camouflaged as adversity. It's worth asking yourself if someone had your identical problems and thrived, what could you be missing?

Encourage yourself by remembering other difficulties you never thought you'd exit, but surprisingly did. Recalling earlier trials is one of the greatest gifts we give ourselves. Avoid analysis paralysis. Talk it out and see ideas materialize. Remember, diamonds don't lie on the soil's surface; they must be dug out. Your answer could be as close as a shovel.

Mining for gold,

Susan M. Watkins

ABOUT THE CONTRIBUTORS

Mary Agrusa authors a weekly blog, *The Thought Just Occurred To Me*, that centers around spiritual issues. She is an award-winning watercolor artist, a musician, and works as a day trader.

M. L. Anderson is a contributing writer for several publications, including all published Christian Authors Guild anthologies. He is a charter member and past president of CAG. Mike formerly worked with the Parable Group of Christian bookstores. Contact him via mlanderson.com.

Theresa Anderson writes, edits, and home educates her two children. Her writing has appeared in *Chicken Soup for the Soul* and *Christian Communicator*. Her family, including eight chickens, resides in the Atlanta area. Contact her at traanderson@gmail.com.

Diana J. Baker is a pastor, worship leader, pianist, teacher, author, and editor. She's served CAG as president, historian, membership director, and hospitality chair and has been published in all CAG anthologies. She's the former editor of *Christian Living* magazine.

Karen Nolan Bell is a writer, actress, musician, artist, and Kentucky mountain storyteller. She writes about her journey through natural disasters, illness, homelessness, eight near-death experiences, and financial ruin in order to give others hope.

Cherise Bopape is an entrepreneur, author, and speaker who enjoys helping women shine personally and professionally. Addressing topics such as parenting, domestic violence, life balance, and communication, Cherise shares her personal struggles and triumphs to inspire women. www.CheriseBopape.net

Mary Bowen holds a master's degree in journalism and has been published in magazines, newspapers, anthologies, and newsletters. She has worked as a newspaper reporter and freelance writer and has served as an editor with the North American Mission Board.

Deborah Crawford is wife, mother, and grandmother to a family that inspires her writing. She leads a Bible study and prayer group. Deborah posts promising messages of hope on her blog at www.mothersforprodigals.com.

Cheryl Anderson Davis was born in Atlanta, raised three children, and was employed over 30 years before starting a new career in writing. She is the author of numerous historical novels.

Frieda Dixon is an author, blogger, and speaker. She writes short stories and has written her memoir, *Born Three Times*. Her blog, www.twolatebloomers.com, encourages senior adults to live life to the fullest.

Vanessa Fortenberry writes inspirational stories for children and adults. She also writes and publishes "Connecting Readers to the Word," a monthly e-newsletter. To learn more about Vanessa, visit her website: http://www.vanessafortenberry.com.

Laura Garron Havens is a retired claim professional reclaiming her bucket-list of to-dos buried in the well of "someday." Hoisting her bucket of unrealized dreams, she plans to pour out inspirational pieces and poetic treasures.

T. W. Lawrence grew up in Texas with one sister, a father who practiced veterinary medicine, and a mother who taught nursing. His family valued the origin and meaning of words. He's written a book of devotionals with a western theme.

Lynn Nester lives in Marietta, GA with her husband of 30 years and their dog that trained them to fetch her blanket for chair-cuddling time. Lynn appreciates good food, good stories, and good friends—not necessarily in that order.

June Parks writes memories of her southern family that had personality and undertook great adventures. Her unforgettable characters offer unrivaled humor. June is an artist, works as a Realtor, and enjoys being a grandmother to five grandkids.

Bryan M. Powell is a composer/arranger with over eighty choral works to his credit. He now enjoys being a full-time novelist. Some of his fourteen faith-based novels were published by Tate Publishing, VaBella Publishing, and Kindle Direct. www.newlifepublicationsonline.com

Sue Schultz is a literature missionary who currently serves as president of the Christian Authors Guild. She enjoys writing devotionals and inspirational stories. Sue is working on a book about mentoring.

Susan Browning Schulz is an author and speaker with works published in *Guideposts*, *Light from the Word*, and other online and print publications. She is co-director of Christian Authors Guild's annual Writers Conference. Visit her blog at www.thelisteningheart.blogspot.com.

Cynthia L. Simmons, speaker, author, and Bible teacher, uses history to encourage women and illustrate biblical truths. Many of her lively presentations come from raising five children and surviving the process.
www.clsimmons.com

Susan M. Watkins is an award-winning multi-published author, formerly writing for CBN's *700 Club* television show. Susan is featured in numerous books, on CBN.com, and in Max Lucado and Gloria Gaynor projects. She's a three-time winner in *Writer's Digest* competitions.

Lynne Watts is a storyteller, speaker, architect of change, and Jesus follower. She is mom to Hayley and Laura and is making a dent in the universe. Lynne is dedicated to a life of service and abundant living. http://acalledwoman.com/

Candy A. Westbrook is a writer and speaker whose passion for Christ lingers on the football field. She uses this canvas as she writes for Southern periodicals to inspire, encourage, share her faith, and point others to the cross. www.helmetkisses.com

ABOUT CHRISTIAN AUTHORS GUILD

Christian Authors Guild embraces writers of various genres who share a common goal: sending a Christian wave upon a secular sea. Meeting twice monthly, the group not only hones the writing skills of its members but also educates and encourages. Members benefit from critique groups, writing contests, monthly seminars, and Christian fellowship.

Each spring, the Christian Authors Guild invites the community to Coffee and Quill—a half-day event where guest speakers share their industry insight with emerging writers. In the fall, the group holds its annual Catch the Wave Writers Conference, where key influencers in the writing and publishing industries teach workshops, accept appointments with conferees, and offer writing tips.

Please visit Christian Authors Guild's website to learn about its other publications, read members' blog posts, or connect with a *Relief Notes* author.

www.ChristianAuthorsGuild.org

Made in the USA
Lexington, KY
22 March 2014